MAKING
CHRISTMAS
CARDS

Judy Balchin

First published in Great Britain 2005

Search Press Limited
Wellwood, North Farm Road,
Tunbridge Wells, Kent TN2 3DR

Text copyright © Judy Balchin 2005

Photographs by Storm Studios

Photographs and design copyright © Search Press Ltd. 2005

ISBN 1 84448 048 8

The Publishers and author can accept no responsibility for any
consequences arising from the information, advice or
instructions given in this publication.

Suppliers
If you have difficulty in obtaining any of the materials and
equipment mentioned in this book, then please visit the
Search Press website for details of suppliers:
www.searchpress.com

Alternatively, you can write to the Publishers at the address
above for a current list of stockists, including firms that
operate a mail-order service.

Publishers' note
All the step-by-step photographs in this book feature the
author, Judy Balchin, demonstrating how to make
Christmas cards. No models have been used.

Manufactured by Classicscan Pte Ltd, Singapore

Printed in Malaysia by Times Offset (M) Sdn Bhd

To Adrian Davies…fish!

Acknowledgements
*I would like to thank John Wright of Pebeo UK
for supplying the glass and silk paints used in this
book. Special thanks go to the supportive team at
Search Press, who as usual have been so helpful
during its writing. In particular, Editorial
Director Roz Dace for her continual guidance;
Felicity Fitchard for her patience and hard work;
Juan Hayward for his creative design skills and
Storm Studios for their photographic skills.
Finally, a big thank you to all you enthusiastic
crafters out there. I hope you enjoy the book.*

Cover
Bejewelled Bethlehem
*Coloured gems and holographic card add sparkle to this
classic glass painted scene.*

Page 1
Twinkling Tree
*Have fun sewing assorted sequins and beads to a felt
Christmas tree.*

Opposite
Wire & Jewel Snowflakes
*Cool colours, snowflake decorations and silver wire and
beads have been used to create a crisp, modern card.*

Contents

Introduction

If, like me, you love Christmas, then this is definitely the book for you. Handmade Christmas cards are fun to make and a joy to receive. The desire to express greetings at Christmas is universal. It is a time to tell those around you just how special they are and what could be more perfect than to make them a handcrafted card.

The sending of a seasonal message goes back a long way, dating as far back as Pagan times when good luck charms were exchanged at the Winter Solstice. Greetings cards have been a huge part of our Christmas celebrations for over a hundred and fifty years. In fact, the first printed Christmas card was created in 1843 by Sir Henry Cole, director of London's Victoria and Albert Museum.

These days, printed cards can be bought inexpensively and are sent in their millions all over the world. In this fast world of mass production, isn't it lovely to receive something just that little bit different, made with care and sent with love?

I have spent many a pleasant hour in a haze of card, sequins and glitter, totally absorbed in creating the Christmas cards in this book and have thoroughly enjoyed every minute of it. I hope to take you with me on a magical journey as you work your way through the projects.

Many of you crafters will have found that your creative talents have guided you through lots of different crafts and this is where this book will help you. Whether it be stitching and embossing, glass or silk painting or just having fun with stickers or wire and beads, there is something for everyone within these pages. You are given simple projects to follow and then shown further card ideas to inspire you. My hope is for you to use this book as a launching pad for your own designs, and for those of you who say that you can't draw – don't worry, patterns are provided throughout the book for every card.

Good luck on your festive journey. Enjoy the adventure and, most importantly, have fun!

Judy

An array of beautiful handmade cards.

Basic materials

You will not need all of the equipment and materials shown on these pages to start your projects. Each individual project provides you with a specific list of requirements for you to look at before you begin.

Pencil Use this to trace designs or to draw them on to card.

Ruler For measuring card, drawing straight lines and, with scissors, to score a fold in a card.

Felt tip pen Useful for tracing around a pattern on to felt or fabric.

Paintbrushes Use a larger brush for applying silk paint to silk (see Seasonal Silk Tree). A smaller paintbrush is used for glass painting (see Festive Fairy) and the detailed painting of the outline sticker (see Bethlehem Sticker Scene).

Scalpel Lift outline stickers with the tip of a scalpel. Use with a **cutting mat** to trim card and paper to the required size.

Scissors Large scissors are used to cut paper, silk and felt. Use small sharp scissors to cut around a painted acetate design (see Festive Fairy) and to score card.

Hole punch Useful for making holes in gift tags for threading with ribbon.

Masking tape Use this for securing patterns and acetate when glass painting (see Festive Fairy). Also use to secure a design behind an aperture card (see Embossed Motifs).

Tracing paper Use this to trace your patterns from the book if a photocopier is not available.

Newspaper Cover your work surface with newspaper when using spray glue. Used for embossing (see Embossed Motifs).

Spray glue For securing papers and silk to card.

Strong glue Such as PVA or superglue. Use this to secure gems, sequins and decorations to a card.

3D foam squares These are used to attach a design panel to a card to give a raised three-dimensional effect. They are also used to keep wire in place when wrapped round a shaped card decoration (see Wire & Bead Star).

General materials for card making

A huge choice of backing card and papers is available nowadays from art and craft shops. This selection includes handmade paper, assorted coloured cards, holographic, mirror and pearlised card, corrugated card, webbing and felt.

Card decorations

Ribbons, coloured cottons, beads, sequins, buttons, gems and
glitter glue can all be used to enhance your cards.

Paints

Silk, glass and watercolour paints are
used in creating some of the cards in
this book. Each project provides you
with a specific list of paints
and colours.

STITCHED STOCKING

You will need:

Red felt, 7 x 12cm
(2¾ x 4¾in)

Pink felt, 3 x 6cm
(1¼ x 2½in)

Pink handmade paper,
9 x 14cm (3½ x 5½in)

Burgundy card,
9 x 14cm (3½ x 5½in)

Gold card, 15 x 20cm
(6 x 7¾in)

Pink and blue
embroidery cottons

Gold glitter glue

Needle

Small blue beads

Felt tip pen

Scissors

Spray glue

Mouse mat

Ruler

Stitching gives this first project that really cosy 'handmade' look. The simple felt stocking is decorated with embroidered stars and glass beads. Remember to keep the basic shape as simple as possible when working in this way, then you can really go to town on the decorative stitching and beadwork. Felt is readily available and comes in a wonderful array of colours. Using contrasting cotton for the stitching and embroidery will make sure that your creation takes pride of place on any mantelpiece at Christmas.

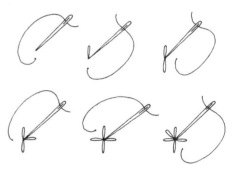

Follow this diagram to create the stitches used on the stocking.

Tip

Felt is perfect for stitching as it does not fray. If you haven't got any, you can stitch on to coloured card.

The template for the Stitched Stocking card.

1. Tear a 5mm (¼in) strip from each edge of the rectangle of handmade paper.

2. Spray the back with spray glue and press it on to the middle of the piece of burgundy card.

3. Photocopy the stocking patterns and cut them out. Lay the paper patterns on to the red felt and draw round the shapes with the felt tip pen.

4. Cut them out.

5. Using strong glue, glue the small rectangular 'cuff' to the top of the stocking.

6. Use the felt tip pen to draw random spots over the stocking as a guide to your embroidery.

7. Using three strands of pink embroidery cotton, thread your needle and knot the end of the thread. Using the diagram on page 8 to help you, sew one star at the top of the stocking.

8. Thread a bead and then push your needle back through the centre of the star. Continue in this way, sewing stars down the felt stocking.

9. Glue the embroidered stocking to the middle of the handmade paper.

10. Lay the panel on a mouse mat. Using your needle, prick stitch holes in the pink paper around the edge of the stocking.

11. Thread your needle with blue embroidery cotton, knot the end and stitch round the stocking.

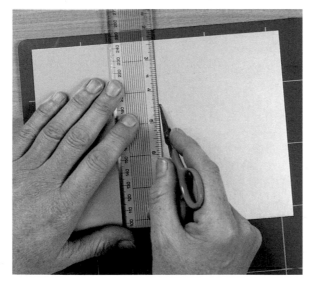

12. Score and fold the gold card down the middle.

13. Glue your stocking panel to the front of the gold card. Add dots of gold glitter glue between the stars. Finally, run a wavy line of glitter glue along the 'cuff' and leave to dry.

The finished Stitched Stocking card.

*Stitching, beads, glitter glue, felt and handmade paper
can be used to make a variety of lovely cards.*

EMBOSSED MOTIFS

You will need:

Silver embossing foil,
10 x 11cm (4 x 4¼in)

Gold card, 6 x 13cm
(2½ x 5in)

Cream card, 21 x 24cm
(8¼ x 9½in)

Gold and silver
ribbons, various widths

Gold star decoration

Ballpoint pen

Pencil and ruler

Scalpel

Cutting mat

Scissors

Newspaper

Piece of scrap paper

Strong glue

Spray glue

Masking tape

And now for something a little more sophisticated. The combination of metal foil and ribbons enclosed in a cream surround gives a crisp, modern feel to this card. Embossing the simple motifs is not difficult but is very effective when combined with the glitzy rows of ribbon and gold card. You are provided with instructions for making the aperture card. Measure and cut it out carefully to achieve a truly professional finish.

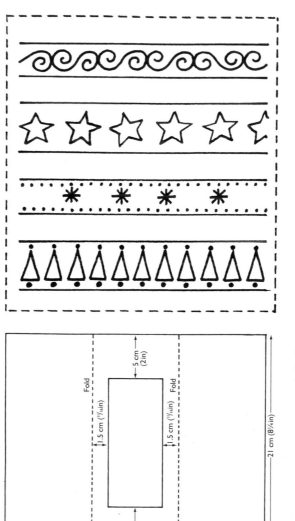

The embossing patterns.

Follow these measurements to create the card.

14

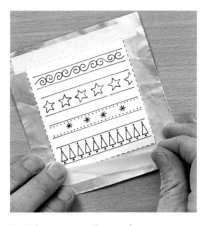

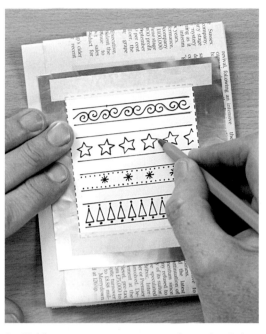

Tip

A ballpoint pen is the perfect tool for creating the embossed lines for this card.

1. Photocopy the embossing pattern and cut it out. Lay the foil face down on your work surface, then tape your pattern on top with some masking tape.

2. Fold up some newspaper and put the foil and the pattern on top. Trace over the pattern with a ballpoint pen.

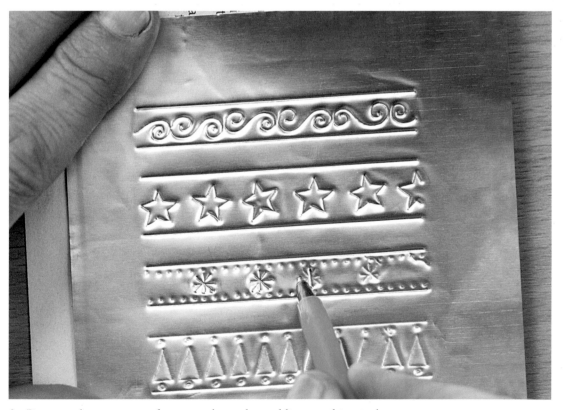

3. Remove the pattern and go over the embossed lines to deepen them.

4. Cut out the embossed strips.

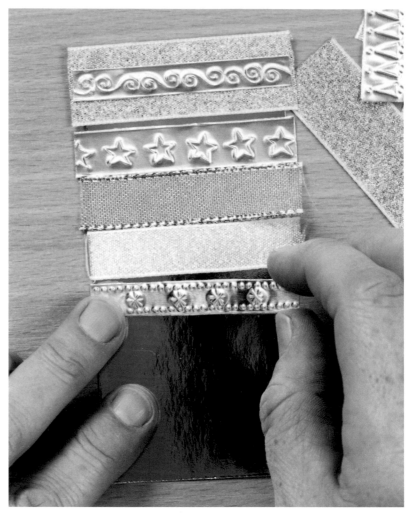

5. Cut some lengths of ribbon the same length as the foil strips. Use the strong glue to glue the strips of foil and the ribbon to the gold card, leaving some spaces so that the gold card can be seen between the strips.

6. Turn the panel over and trim off the overhanging foil and ribbon.

7. Using the diagram on page 14 to help you, measure and pencil in the fold lines and aperture on the cream card. Score the folds with scissors and cut out the aperture.

8. Cut a 2mm ($^{1}/_{16}$in) strip from the left-hand edge of the card.

9. Tape your decorated panel face down behind the aperture with strips of masking tape.

10. Cover the right-hand third of your cream card with a piece of scrap paper. Spray the remaining card with spray glue.

11. Fold the left-hand flap over and press to secure.

12. Turn the card over and glue a gold star to the middle of your decorated panel.

The finished Embossed Motifs card.

You can create lots of different shapes and patterns for cards with embossing.

SEASONAL SILK TREE

You will need:

Habotai silk, 12 x 18cm
(4¾ x 7in)

Emerald green and
turquoise silk paints

Tube of gold gutta

Thick white card,
5.5 x 12cm
(2¼ x 4¾in)

Blue card, 15 x 18cm
(6 x 7in)

Gold card, 6 x 12.5cm
(2½ x 5in)

Red glitter glue

Star decoration

Masking tape

Paintbrush

Scissors

Pencil

Sheet of polythene

Newspaper

Spray glue

Iron

If you love messing about with paints, then this project is definitely for you. Colouring the silk is great fun and no two cards will ever be the same with this technique. The simple tree design is piped over the coloured silk with gold gutta. The addition of a glittery pot, baubles and a shining star will ensure that your friends will be delighted to display this mini masterpiece.

The template for the Seasonal Silk Tree card.

1. Immerse the piece of silk in water and squeeze out the excess. Lay the crumpled wet silk on the sheet of polythene.

2. Dot on emerald silk paint with a paintbrush.

3. Repeat with the turquoise colour.

4. Turn the crumpled silk over and repeat, making sure that the silk is completely coloured. Leave to dry.

Tip

The wet silk can be dried with a hair dryer. Place it under a sieve or colander while drying to prevent it from blowing away.

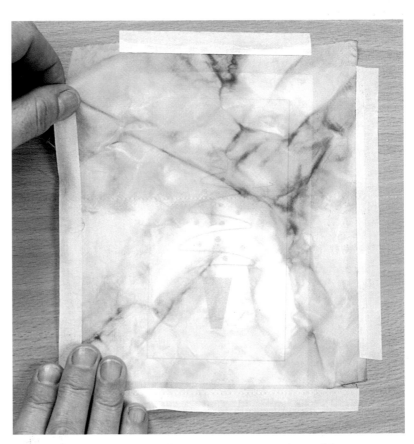

5. Iron the silk. Photocopy the pattern, cut around it and lay it on your work surface. Spread the silk out and, using masking tape, tape it down over the pattern, making sure it is stretched taut.

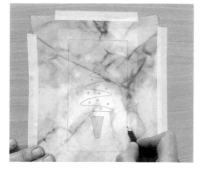

6. Trace the pattern with a pencil. Do not trace the star.

7. Remove the masking tape and cut out the silk rectangle. Lay it on some newspaper and spray the back of the silk lightly with spray glue.

8. Lay the card rectangle in the middle of the silk and cut away the corners as shown.

9. Fold the silk over the edges as shown, making sure they stick securely.

10. Score and fold the blue card down the middle. Glue the gold card to the front of the blue card.

11. Glue your painted silk panel to the front of the card.

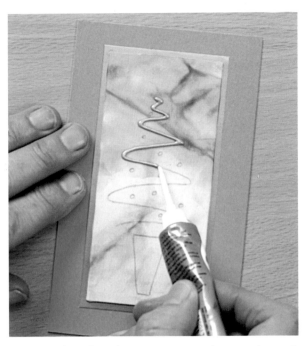

12. Use the tube of gutta to pipe in the wavy line of the Christmas tree.

13. Add baubles and a plant pot using glitter glue.

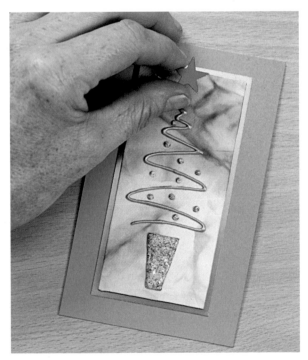

14. Glue the star decoration just above the tree and leave to dry.

The finished Seasonal Silk Tree card.

Experiment with various paint colours to achieve different effects.

WIRE & BEAD STAR

You will need:

Pearl lilac card,
10.5 x 21cm
(4¼ x 8¼in) and a
8.5cm (3½in) square

Pink handmade paper,
5.5 x 9cm (2¼ x 3½in)

Iridescent star
decoration

1 metre of silver wire

Pink beads

3D foam squares

Spray glue

Scissors

Scalpel

Cutting mat

Ruler

If, like me, you hoard crafty bits and bobs gathered here and there as you trawl the craft shops, then you will definitely want to have a go at this project. With a little wire, card, handmade paper and some beads, you can create a very stylish card indeed. Colour schemes are important. The bright pink beads combine well with the vibrant handmade paper and the more subtle pearlised lilac card. The iridescent star is ready made, but can easily be reproduced with the template below.

The template for the star.

1. Glue the star decoration to the square of lilac card. Use a ruler and scalpel to cut around the edge so that it has a 2mm ($^1/_{16}$in) border of lilac card all around the star.

2. Press 3D foam squares to the back of the star and remove the backing papers.

3. Attach one end of the wire on to the back of the 3D foam squares.

4. Bring the wire round to the front and thread on a few beads.

Tip

Lay your small beads ready for threading on a piece of cloth to prevent them from rolling away.

5. Take the wire around to the back again.

6. Continue in this way until you have wrapped the wire around five times to create an inner beaded star shape.

7. Press the wire on to the 3D foam squares and trim the end to neaten.

8. Cut a3D foam square to make five small squares and add to each point of the star. Put to one side.

10. Glue the handmade paper to the left-hand side of the front of the card.

9. Tear a 5mm (¼in) strip from the right-hand edge of the handmade paper.

11. Press the finished star decoration on to the front of the lilac card base, lining up the top of the star with the edge of the torn handmade paper.

The finished Wire & Bead Star card.

Opposite: The wire can be curled to create a ribbon effect on gifts and trailing stars.

FESTIVE FAIRY

Time to get out those glass paints and have some fun. Take a little time to practise using the outliner tube on paper first. Practice makes perfect as they say and the aim is to achieve an even, unbroken line. Painting your fairy is great fun but you may want to dilute some of the more dense paints with clear glass paint to lighten the colour, as light will not be shining through the design. Backing the painted acetate design with holographic card adds a real sparkle to your festive friend!

The template for the Festive Fairy card.

1. Photocopy the pattern, cut around it and tape it to the piece of thick white card. Tape the acetate over the pattern.

2. Use the tube of outliner to outline the design. Leave to dry.

3. Lift up the acetate and remove the pattern underneath. Retape the acetate to the white card.

4. Paint the fairy's hair and wings with yellow paint.

5. Paint the dress and shoes in red.

Tip

Apply the paint generously so that it settles flat within the outlined area.

6. Paint the cuffs and dress hem in orange.

7. Mix some clear glass paint and a spot of orange for the skin areas.

8. Mix a pale turquoise for the background.

9. Paint the border in green. Leave to dry.

11. Spray the back of the acetate with spray glue and stick the acetate fairy to the holographic card.

10. Cut around the design carefully.

12. Fold the red card and glue the fairy design to the front.

13. Glue some red gems to the fairy's dress hem.

14. Add some silver stars to the turquoise background.

The finished Festive Fairy card.

Try adding beads, jewels and stickers to create fun details on your cards.

BETHLEHEM STICKER SCENE

Outline stickers really do take all the hard work out of card making. Just peel them off, stick them down and then decorate them with paints. Vibrant silk paints are used to paint this Bethlehem scene, giving it a rich glow; just right for Christmas. Alternatively, watercolours can be used. Colours can be painted flat or blended within each section to give the design more depth. Some of the stars from the sticker sheet are used to decorate the co-ordinating ribbon hanging from the main design.

The Bethlehem outline sticker.

1. Use a scalpel to peel the sticker away from the backing sheet. Leave it to rest for a minute to regain its shape. Press it on to the watercolour paper.

2. Paint each section with water before applying the paint. This makes it easier to blend the colours.

3. Paint the hills in yellow and, while the paint is still wet, add a little raspberry and blend it in for shading.

4. Paint the paths, steps and buildings with iris, turquoise and cyan. Paints can be mixed together on a palette or diluted with water to create different hues and shades.

5. For the palm tree trunks, mix yellow and raspberry to create a dark orange colour.

6. Paint the upper part of the sky with cyan. While the paint is still wet, fill in the lower half with raspberry.

7. When dry, press small outline stars on to the sky area and trim around the design.

8. Glue the piece of ribbon to the back of the design.

10. Glue the square of mirror card on top of the webbing.

11. Apply some 3D foam squares on to the back of your design and remove the backing papers.

9. Spray glue the glitter webbing and press it on to the front of the card blank.

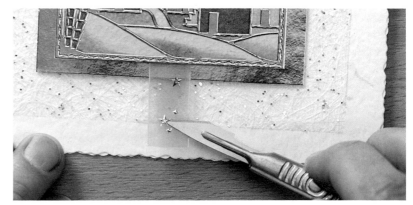

12. Press the design on to the mirror card.

13. Press some small sticky stars on to the tail of ribbon.

41

The finished Bethlehem Sticker Scene card.

Opposite: There are various outline stickers available to try on your cards.

Templates

Stitched Stocking variations (see page 13)

*These templates are
shown full size.*

Embossed Motifs variations (see page 19)

These templates are shown full size.

Seasonal Silk Tree variations (see page 25)

These templates are shown full size.

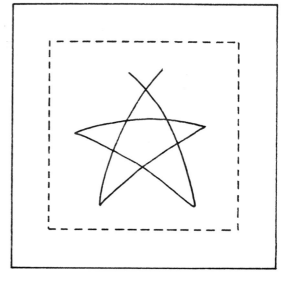

Wire & Bead Star variations (see page 31)

*These templates are shown half size.
You will need to enlarge them 100%
on a photocopier.*

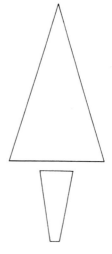

Festive Fairy variations (see page 37)

*These templates are shown half size.
You will need to enlarge them 100%
on a photocopier.*

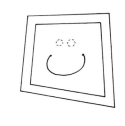

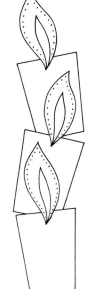

Front cover

*This template is shown half size. You
will need to enlarge it 100% on a
photocopier.*

Index

Festive felt crown
Recreate this fun gift tag using felt, handmade paper, silver glitter glue, silver ribbon, blue and white card, silver beads and metallic blue embroidery cotton.